Swift River Ballad

Swift River Ballad

Poems by

Thomas DeFreitas

Cover design by Shay Culligan.
Cover photo by Kazuend on Unsplash (unsplash.com/@kazuend).
Author photo by Mary Buchinger. Used with permission.

ISBN: 978-1-63980-416-0

Kelsay Books
502 South 1040 East, A-119
American Fork, Utah 84003
Kelsaybooks.com

for Elena Lee Johnson
poet and friend

Acknowledgments

Poems which have previously appeared in journals, whether print or online, include the following:

Autumn Sky Poetry Daily: "She, Barkeep, to Him, Barfly"

The Christendom Review: "I do not approve" (as "Le Poète Maudit")

Mudfish: "Sickness and Health"

The Orchards: "Photograph"

Plainsongs: "Flowers" (as "And Flowers"), "I could learn from him"

Red Letter Poems: "Swift River Ballad" (poems for RLP are chosen and electronically circulated by Steven Ratiner, Poet Laureate Emeritus of Arlington, MA)

The Somerville Times: "Dreaming of Somerville," "La Danseuse"; "Working Girls"

Soul-Lit: "Littles, Lie More Close!" (as "98th Letter to Elena"

*

Sincerest thanks to Karen Kelsay, to Delisa Hargrove, to Jenna Wray, and to the entire team at Kelsay Books for their courtesy, diligence, patience, and continued hospitality to my work. Special gratitude to Shay Culligan for his professional attention to the design of the cover.

To Jennifer Martelli, David P. Miller, and Christie Towers: You bless me by your kind words for this collection! I am duly grateful.

The New England Poetry Club (with co-presidents Doug Holder and Denise Provost) continues to be a dynamo of good service to our noble and vitalizing art. I am especially indebted to my "sibs from other cribs," Hilary Sallick and Mary Buchinger, for their luminous example and loyal friendship.

I am in constant awe of James Parker, John Lane, Christie Towers, Rev. Jennifer McCracken, and all the St. Paul's Cathedral staff who make the Tuesday gatherings of the Black Seed Writers possible. Amazing things happen in Sproat Hall!

To Arlington's poet laureate, Jean Flanagan, and to her predecessors, Steven Ratiner, Cathie Desjardins, and Miriam Levine: a tip of the hat, a bow of the head, and so much more!

To my family of faith and love at St. James's Episcopal Church, Cambridge; to our invaluable rector, Rev. Matthew Stewart; to our indefatigable music minister, Patrick Michaels; to co-parishioners too numerous to name: you are my cherished kith and kin.

Elena Lee Johnson, thank you for allowing me to dedicate this book to you! You are a light.

Alisha De Freitas, *sorella mia:* I am fortified always by your High Church Anglican Black Panther prayers!

Steven Riddle, friend who knows (and often speaks!) my mind, you are the gentle Rid Vicious to my tame Tommy Rotten!

Deborah S. Briggs, thank you wholeheartedly. You know me better than God does!

Heather Lynn Fairfield, thank you wholesouledly. You know me better than God does!

Lisa Williams, for all your kindnesses over the years, I owe you at least one universe. You are awesomeness epitomized.

Jen Toler, dear friend, your light has not been and will never be extinguished. I miss you sorely, and I love you lots.

To John, Ingrid, Sue, Perry, Kenny, Elizabeth: you are wise and kind, and you give me hope.

To Tammi, Whitney, Sarah, Amy, Ashley, and so many others, *merci.* We are indeed the luckiest.

Jenny DeFreitas, my beekeeper cousin! Always adept at keepin' things buzzin'! You are a perpetual grace.

Dad, I'm hoping it's wonderfully mellow up there.

Mom, as always, big hug. Bushel and a peck. (That coffee's got coffee in it.)

Peace and light to all of you who are holding and reading these pages.

Contents

Autumnography

It's in the gallow-palaver
of trees, the undermutter
of stiffening leaves,

in the burnt flavor
of late afternoon air.
Sly rake of the wind,

October's insinuation
in the scowling brow
of westering sunlight.

Furtive now, clandestine,
whisper-witted gestures,
but soon enough: blatant,

reckless flamboyance,
spending fire-colors
in a glorious death-gamble.

Dreaming of Somerville

for Lloyd Schwartz

I dream of shining fish, slow and sleek,
swimming the murk of the Mystic.

I dream of murals in Brickbottom,
graffiti at Walnut and Pearl.

I dream of slender mysterious poems
kept in Nana's pantry on the second floor
of the house on Laurel Terrace.

I dream of the face of God on the Number 80 bus,
the feet of God in dollar-store flip-flops,
the arms of God lugging groceries up Spring Hill.

I dream of cool September nights,
of festivals in August,
of akathists and litanies,
the bells of the Dormition.

I dream of College Avenue,
alive with a thousand undergraduates
and bright with banners of Pride.

I dream of Tony's Spa, long gone.
I dream of the Burren, the Sligo.
I dream of Renée's Café.

I dream of summer-limber dancers
lindyhopping in Davis Square
on a golden and danceworthy Saturday.

I dream of the Little Sisters of the Poor.
I dream of the Lost Bookstore.
I dream of the Armory.

Elegy

in memory of Dolores O'Riordan (1971–2018)

Every lost child
weeps with Dolores,
little girl prisoned
in a world of winter,
fragile doll-body
in a globe of snow.
Glass smithereens
against slate-grey rocks.
She reels from a pain
against which her angel
did not protect her.

Every living voice
sings with Dolores,
Queen of Limerick,
Lady of Sorrows,
fierce as Freya
when she's at the guitar,
brave as St. Brigid,
this whiskey soprano,
this pint-sized fighter.

Every parched spirit
drinks with Dolores
from a well of solace,
from a lake of grace
pure as the first star
kindled in Genesis,
wide as the mantle
of the sheltering Virgin.

Every bright body
dances with Dolores
whose exultant feet
kiss wondering earth,
who sways in the night,
leans into the breeze,
whose hymnody glimmers
in ghostly moonglow,
whose triumphs and tears
are stored in a bottle,
kept in a book.

Flowers

April brings baseball, "Sweet Caroline," and flowers.
May gets drunk on the purple wine of flowers.

We practice *nepsis,* wakeful expectation—
Wait for rain and the first sweet sign of flowers.

PLEASE LOVE WHAT GROWS HERE, urges a placard,
Greek to the prowling beasts who dine on flowers.

In Fr. McNichols' *Gate of Heaven* icon,
Christ holds the modest columbine, O flowers.

A ladybug, that spotted token of luck,
Creeps meek among the stems and spines of flowers.

Wreathed in dreams and secrets, Oscar Wilde
Often sought the anodyne of flowers.

When can we forsake our occupations,
Roll in lush clover, laze, recline in flowers?

The trellis outside this suburban demesne
Is graced with a trailing vine of flowers.

Georgia O'Keeffe wrought massive canvases:
With labial petals, she'd design her flowers.

Poetic adolescent, teenage Springsteen,
Amid East Boston's rust, you pine for flowers.

The sacristan adorns the orient chapel
With incense, icons (Byzantine!), and flowers.

Quirk-witted Thomas, abbot of Amplegirth,
Surprise your lively valentine with flowers!

Her Mind, Her Heart

for Mary, for Hilary

Her mind
is intricate
as *Celosia cristata,*
agile as a Calder-creation,
shapely as a candled shrine
beside a road in Arizona,
as luminous as 1983,
as strong as gossamer
withstanding gales,
her mind is bright
as a raindrop
beading the end
of a summer branch,
expressive
as Miss Moore's
understatements,
acrobatic as meditation,
antic as stillness,
fertile as a community garden,
imperishable as the moon's
tear-tarnished silver,
companionable as a blanket
on the first snowy night
of November:
an anchorite, a stylite,
a Dickinsonian
frog in a bog,
a sparrow swifter
than any search engine,
a sister to all who seek
solace, strength.

*

Her heart
weighs all life
in a love-balance:
her wit-bright eyes
surpass the sagacity
of Lao-tzu
and the Synoptics;
her sandalled footsteps
chant litanies
to the waking earth;
her subtle smile
coaxes laughter
from the backyards
and paving-stones
of a metaphysical
Somerville,
where pigeons
recite scripture
to the windows
of triple-deckers
and an overfed cat
curls purringly
around the ankles
of a poet who keeps
the trails of shooting stars
in her generous
chevelure.

I could learn from him

His handsome poem
ambles down the page
in workboots, khakis,
and a corduroy vest.

Doesn't need rhyme
any more than a lilac
needs cologne, or Jesus
needs televangelists.

Might be having a
bad day. Shrugs it off,
and gets on with the
business at hand.

I do not approve

But I do not approve. And I am not resigned.
—Edna St. Vincent Millay, "Dirge Without Music"

I do not approve of death
Unless it is sensual,
Something forbidden, ecstatic
Entered into.
A sweet desideratum and delight.
The torpidinal
Stygian kisses
Of an ageless avatar.

I will not venture into love
Unless it is secular,
Some stultifying wine or water
Swallowed.
Astonishing intoxicant!
The vertiginal
Liquid image
Of a masterful tempter.

I cannot accept hostility
Unless it is intimate,
The armor of the adversary's heart
Removed.
A flesh-and-bone opponent.
The original
Unguarded body
Of a redoubtable warrior.

I write because

for Beth Kress

I write because, at the front of Room 214, Mr. Waldron had a poster of "The Road Not Taken," complete with bare brown tree and forked black path.

I write because I needed to fill up the time in study hall and didn't feel like studying.

I write because of Don McLean, The Looking Glass, America, Lennon & McCartney.

I write because what else was an only child to do who couldn't throw a football, shoot baskets, hit home runs, score goals?

I write because Joseph, Erin, Emily, Alison, and Marzieh have been my therapists. Because Barry, Peggy, Clara, Steve, and Gusti have guided my spirit wisely.

I write because of tired faces on the Red Line. Because of black coffee and Dylan Thomas.

I write because Brother Pat Logan played "Let It Be" on his guitar in the Salesian Boys Club chapel.

I write because of Hart Crane, because of Franconia Notch, because of cold showers and ambidextrous crushes.

I write because of Saint Lucie's Day, *the yeares mid-night.*

I write because of *Wishes, Lies, and Dreams.* Because of Seamus Heaney and Juan de la Cruz.

I write because Tracy Chapman smote my heart at first sight. Because Cardinal Bergoglio would become Pope Francis.

I write because Paul Ashman killed a spider in his backyard, and we buried it under a small mound of dirt, and said Catholic prayers to ensure its sweet repose.

I write because of insomnia and even more black coffee. I write like Wystan Auden's bastard child.

I write for the woman who, years ago at Uncle Bob's barbecue, looked at me funny when I said I was 29 and not married.

I write because Dr. Macmillan made me better, Dr. Naidoo made me worse.

I write because E. E. Cummings grew up in Cambridge and is buried in Jamaica Plain. Because Uta Pippig won the hundredth Boston Marathon.

I write: Simple Minds, The Smiths, New Order, Depeche Mode, The Cure, The Fixx, The Jam, The Call, The Clash, The Fall, Dexys Midnight Runners, A Flock of Seagulls.

I write because nobody's stopped me yet.

La Danseuse

at u mass amherst
near the fine arts center

the tie-dyed undergrad

young woman of lavish hair
and willowy figure

sways barefoot
to the pulsing music
of the outdoor concert

her ten pale toes
churning
scrumptious mud

Lake

Untarnishable coin
on the North Country's
old rough fabric,
shiny startlement
amid miles of steep
meanderings, you
mirror the moon's
cold gape and gleam.

A ripple of light
trembles your skin
to a quick felicity,
titanic teardrop
nestled in the pock
and crease of earth.

Littles, Lie More Close!

Hornet's nest
on my porch.
Hope it's dormant.

*

Branches greening,
proclaiming April!
Why am I testy?

*

Beneath her tread,
plush grass
aches with love.

*

Could you be
prouder, louder—
daffodil?

*

Muddy reek
as sun-warmed earth
softens, unclenches.

*

Someone says her name.
His old-man heart
does cartwheels.

A Mad Patch of Song

You are the pink mint of floral days.
Pert froth of comic blossoms, sip
of cool blue heaven. You are the trust
of once-braided hair flaunting in a breeze.
Who can compass your gestures and jests
against the green tedium of summer?

Iris among ferns in the dank hollow.
Accidental majesty no curse can hurt.
I will greet you with a mad patch
of song. And you will brighten and blush,
crash into a racket of laughter, nudge me
out of the dust into rainburst and radiance.

Match Game

I was a curious boy of eight, watching
Match Game. Suspecting something juicy,
I was chuckling at the word "bisexual,"

filling in a blank. Mom asked if I
knew what the word meant. I admitted
I didn't. She told me, "It's somebody

who likes both boys *and* girls." She
paused before adding, "It's against
the Catholic Church." I wondered why

such open-heartedness would merit a
frosty *No!* from Paul our pope, Humberto
our bishop, Fr. Wilson, Fr. Piscatelli—

but I didn't have a language then
to dress my doubts and questions in.

My belly

is ample and accepting, catholic and capacious; it takes up space, it gives you room: my big old liberal belly, filled with poached eggs and coffee, subversive stories and baritone dollops of whimsy.

Today I am thanking my belly for being so well-rounded: truly, a civil and impeccable gentlebelly, eager with factoids, brave with bombast, adroit at a quadrillion gaucheries. No joke! There's nothing prim or diminutive about my belly.

Sonnets plead to be composed, given voice and vigor, praising the span and scope of my belly, comic whippersnapper, surly bastard.

Miraculous mischief becomes my belly; all things coarse and calamitous dwell within its domain: glittering visitors present their credentials at my endomorphic court.

My belly is Massachusetts and Mannahatta; pacific and pedantic, it pays effusive homage to other bellies of its phylum and ilk.

Winsome and tickled. Athletic as a boulder. Chaste as a film-noir vixen. My belly sings Ambrosian canticles, tells brash and lascivious jokes.

Behold the half-assed majesty, the off-kilter lean and lilt of my belly. It stands at the door of the five-and-ten, it kneels at your Converse high-tops, kisses you on the instep, and makes you feel quite larkish and daft.

November

for Anne McMaster

darkforked treescape   growth crisped brittle
blossoms are withered   pollen is history

for a season and a season   the fragrant frost
dustflurry   dandruffsnow   iceflowers

spent leaves heaped on the devil's strip
rainmade mud amid deathstones

downfall   windfall   firefall

stumbling glories   museblaze
of mortal splendour   unsummering hills

the year nods off   dusk a pebbletoss
from noon   blight and blast of northwind

bones steeped in chill
puffs of vapor on damp days

what shrine more venerable than this grey
this wink toward winter

hearth-gather   harvest-hoard   cider-huddle
to thole   to muddle through   to thrive

Photograph

Ruins of a Cistercian abbey.
Summer's heat greens
the cloister-wreck.

A low stone wall
out of Frost's blank verse
winds beside a stooped elm.

Grass, moss, ivy
(heedless, creedless)
claim these saint-acres as their own,

this church of ghost-stone
whose time-bitten archway's
blazing with strong low sun.

She, Barkeep, to Him, Barfly

both retired from their positions

Sometimes you'd really get to me, y'know?
Fifty-cent vocab and a slacker's gut,
you'd guzzle Newcastle 'til you browned out
on that barstool you wore your cheek-prints into.

Ridiculous tipper! No, you'd never stiff me,
but Jesus, *forty percent?* Dude, you must've
wanted me more than the dark English stout
you'd gulp down to dial back your lovestruck fluster.

I gave you grief. You took it straight, no chaser,
never flinching from my ashtray trash-talk,
my moods as changeable as late October.

I miss you sometimes, bro. You weren't a jerk.
And I know I could be a piece of work.
And hey, good luck, I heard you're getting sober.

Sickness and Health

after John Ashbery

New stirrings lie ahead
For the last great apostle of rugged individualism.
Forty years in captivity
Slide by. You write poems
About the paper seagull, the clockwork sea.
A grim stamp of validation rises
Like a daisy-colored moon
Over the lackluster sward, over
Mechanical ponds where ducks
Quack and flutter, brushing the air
With minimal, bombastic strokes.

What do you hear, what do you say?
I think I shall do nothing
For the rest of my life but listen
To your breath,
Yes, breathe your airs and glances.
Suppose I asked you
To have a heart, would you
Think it a rude request?

No one speaks.
The self-spending moon conks out.
The lavish ocean drowses.

Swallow, Come Flying

for Elena, after Bishop and Neruda

From acres of corn and untrafficked railroads
to the scrambled eggs and bacon of Andy's Diner,
from the flora and fauna of Forgottonia
to the collects and antiphons of St. James's Church,
fly with palpable blessings under your wings!

From bicycle-paths, from American Family Field,
from the Menomonee and the Hank Aaron Trail,
to the bookstores of Harvard Square,
to the ghosts of Elsie's, the Tasty, the Wursthaus,
fly with golden diplomas and luminous degrees!

From the weather-tilted barn where bats flit in the hayloft
to Cooke's Hollow, to the old mill brook
between police headquarters and the Eversource plant,
fly with your peerless spiritual radar!

From birthday parties, from floral Domes,
to moondancing drinks at the Druid Pub,
from the winsome baristas of Stone Creek
to the dulcet-strumming buskers of Brattle Street,
fly with coffee-beans, spare change, sheet music,
fly with metaphysics, with hard Midwestern rain!

From "Amazing Grace" and "Nearer My God to Thee"
to "Losing My Religion" and "Closer to Fine,"
fly with human hymnals! fly with taciturn blackbirds!

From the dactyls of didactic quarterlies
to tabloids blaring life's quotidian toxicity,
fly with crimson proverbs, with actual azure epigrams!

From seesaws, monkeybars, swingsets,
to secret painted tunnels under Somerville thoroughfares,
fly with shining Saturdays of art, music, dance!

Fly with humble grace into our precincts,
fly with your heart of hyacinths into Logan,
soar through crystal heights, sail on the breeze,
piper and troubadour of clearest morning poems!

Swift River Ballad

A winter sky darkens above Swift River;
Regulars gather at Charlie's Bar & Grill.
"I Fall to Pieces" plays on the old jukebox
Beside the grudge-handled cigarette machine.

Regulars gather at Charlie's Bar & Grill:
There's a faint smell of sawdust and spent dreams.
Beside the grudge-handled cigarette machine,
A grit-voiced redhead staggers from cheap gin.

There's a faint smell of sawdust and spent dreams:
Five or six local boys get high out back.
A grit-voiced redhead staggers from cheap gin:
Who's gonna buy the lady another drink?

Five or six local boys get high out back:
Money is scarce and jobs are hard to come by.
Some guy buys Julianne another drink—
Larry, that's Butch's kid, his wife just left him . . .

Money is scarce and jobs are hard to come by:
"I Fall to Pieces" plays on the old jukebox.
Like a comfortless man whose wife's just left him,
A winter sky darkens above Swift River.

That Old Song Again

a golden shovel for Carmellite Chamblin

Happenstance and Circumstance, the
meek-fleeced sheep I count as I lie in bed
at the outset of my second half-century of

shame and roses, embarrassment and lilies,
nagging ohs and vexed exes plastered across
the tic-tac-toe grid of my life: memories, the

rambunctious neighbors down the street
who engineer drastic surprises: poked
ribs, milked jokes, well-aimed potshots at my

amour propre, and yikes! my mind's desire
to dance with wind-whipt October leaves, to
belt out power-ballads at Wembley, to be

a dangerous example to my pals and gals, a
monk *manqué,* the mentally unkempt child
of two carefree kids, yes, that old song again.

Thursday Night Meeting

in memory of J. L. T.

The women of the Thursday night meeting
have eyes as lively as a hockey brawl,
hearts tough as sparrows, tender as men.
Their feet are tired from ten-hour workdays,
their bones as weary as trampled grass;
their spirits as resilient as music, as April.

The women of the Thursday night meeting
(once too young, too cool for their own good,
now settled into canny middle age)
sit knitting—blankets, scarves.
With one dapper man among them,
also knitting: fortunate, absorbed.

They call themselves the Luscious Lushes.
They drink ghastly black coffee
as the old truck-driver,
red jaw stubbled grey,
breaks down giving a share
that tells of his reuniting
with a long-estranged daughter
soon to be married.

The women know these stories.
They've lived them.

They work their program:
They've read the Big Book,
prayed the Serenity Prayer;
they're always reaching out.
In her Newport 100 voice,
Melissa brags:

"I've been to more churches
than the Pope, God bless him!"

Pray for me, women hurting and healing,
triumphant in your trials, wise and strong and kind,
women humble-hearted and higher-powered:
teach me a tenth of your patient endurance.

The Widow at Ninety

Brian was a good man. Born
in Tipperary, he came here with
his parents when he was thirteen.
Served in the Navy during Korea.

We got married in '54, at St. Ann's
on Holcomb Road. It's closed now.
He died of a heart attack, my Brian.
Only forty-two. I was suddenly left

to raise four boys by myself. I had to
learn how to pay the bills. I did it!
Would you like another cup of tea?
No trouble! Oh, I miss him—still!

He always did the shopping, not me.
He was a better cook than I was,
and believe you me, I'm no slouch!
Not once did he ever hit me or the kids.

Working Girls

I have never known your pain,
never felt your weariness
of life's treatment, of the traffic
and trade of precious things
survival can sometimes entail.
I honor your endurance.
I would soothe your anguish,
give deep sleep to your tired eyes,
calm your nerves, hush your fears.

And I would do still more:
I would raise you to the altars
of a new church, where the last
truly are the first, where power
kneels to destitution, where men
applauded for their righteousness
crouch down and, weeping, wash the feet
of women whom they used to deem
beyond redemption's reach.

Notes

"Autumnography": Gregory Corso's poem "Of One Month's Reading of English Newspapers" contains the verse "And autumnographers wage their agriculture."

"Flowers": William Hart McNichols (b. 1949) is a priest and iconographer from Denver, currently resident in New Mexico.

"I could learn from him": *Him* is Ted Kooser, the former US Poet Laureate (b. 1939; term as laureate, 2004-06).

"I do not approve": *torpidinal,* from the noun "torpedo."

"I write because": Written after having read a draft of Beth Kress's agile, adroit, accomplished poem "Why I Write." See her collection *Taking Notes* (Finishing Line Press, 2020).

"Littles, Lie More Close!": Theodore Roethke's poem "In Evening Air" contains the line "Ye littles, lie more close!"

"Match Game": Cardinal Humberto S. Medeiros (1915–83) was the Roman Catholic Archbishop of Boston from 1970 until his death.

"November": *Devil's strip* (American Midwest), a margin of grass found between a sidewalk and the asphalt of the street. *To thole* (Northern Ireland): to endure.

"Swallow, Come Flying": the Milwaukee-based poet Elena Lee Johnson often signs herself *barn swallow.* My poem to Elena is modelled on Pablo Neruda's "Alberto Rojas Jiménez Comes Flying" and Elizabeth Bishop's "Invitation to Miss Marianne Moore."

"That Old Song Again": The 15 end-words form a line from the poem "July 1, 2018" by the Boston-based poet Carmellite Chamblin.

About the Author

Thomas DeFreitas was born in Boston, was educated at the Boston Latin School, and attended the University of Massachusetts in Boston and in Amherst. His poems have appeared in *Autumn Sky Poetry Daily, Dappled Things, Ibbetson Street, Pensive, Plainsongs, Red Letter Poems,* and elsewhere.

Thomas's poem "Chasing the Waves" was chosen by Arlington (MA) Poet Laureate Cathie Desjardins to be part of the Talking Chair Project, an interactive poetry exhibit installed during April 2018 at the Robbins Library in Arlington. In the summer of 2019, "Detox" was chosen as an Award Poem by the editors of *Plainsongs.* Thomas's début collection, *Winter in Halifax,* was published by Kelsay Books in 2021. The following year, Kelsay released Thomas's second poetry book, *Longfellow, Tell Me.*

Several hymns with words by Thomas DeFreitas and music by Patrick Michaels ("Her Name Is Grace"; "Restore Our Life") have recently been performed as part of the eucharistic liturgy at St. James's Episcopal Church in Cambridge, Massachusetts.

A resident of Arlington, Massachusetts since 2010, Thomas is an associate member of the Academy of American Poets. He is also active in the New England Poetry Club, Boston's Black Seed Writers' Group, and Arlington's Bee Hive Poets.

Website:
thomasdefreitas.me

www.ingramcontent.com/pod-product-compliance
Lightning Source LLC
Chambersburg PA
CBHW031009090426
42737CB00008B/739